# HOW TO MONETIZE

"How To Make Money From TikTok, Instagram, Facebook, Twitter, WordPress, LinkedIn, Twitch, YouTube, And OKE.IO. Guide To Marketing Strategies, Promotion And Financial Success."

By

**RIZE JENKINS**

# TABLE OF CONTENTS

**CHAPTER ONE** ................................................................................................. 5
    What is social media monetization? ................................................................. 5
    Why you should monetize social media ......................................................... 6
    Defining your niche ........................................................................................ 6
    Monetize-social-media ................................................................................... 7

**CHAPTER TWO** ................................................................................................ 8
    How to monetize Tok-tok .............................................................................. 8
    How much money can you make from TikTok? ........................................... 16
    Does TikTok pay creators for videos? ......................................................... 16

**CHAPTER THREE** ......................................................................................... 20
    How to Monetize Your Instagram ................................................................ 20
    How do I grow my Instagram? .................................................................... 21
    Practical tactics to monetize your Instagram ............................................... 23
    Monetize your Instagram with different tactics and platforms ..................... 26

**CHAPTER FOUR** ........................................................................................... 29
    How to Make Money on Facebook .............................................................. 29
    Make Money with Your Twitter Account ................................................... 35

**CHAPTER FIVE** ............................................................................................. 38
    How To Monetize Your WordPress Website .............................................. 38
    What is WordPress? .................................................................................... 39
    WordPress.com vs WordPress.org ............................................................... 39
    What You Need to Monetize Your Website ................................................ 39

Why you need to Make Money from Your Website ............................................................. 40

How to Make Money on WordPress: The Strategies ......................................................... 40

## CHAPTER SIX ................................................................................................................. 45

How To Monetize Your LinkedIn Account ......................................................................... 45

Requirements for monetization ............................................................................................ 45

Earning from LinkedIn .......................................................................................................... 46

## CHAPTER SEVEN ............................................................................................................ 49

How to Make Money on Twitch ........................................................................................... 49

Income Sources Available to Twitch Partners Only ........................................................... 55

## CHAPTER EIGHT ............................................................................................................. 56

How to Earn Money from YouTube Channel ..................................................................... 57

Who Can Upload Videos on YouTube? ............................................................................... 57

How to Check the Total Number of Subscribers ................................................................ 60

How to Check the Total Watch Time .................................................................................. 60

How to Check Channel Strike Status .................................................................................. 61

## CHAPTER NINE ............................................................................................................... 64

How to monetize OKE.IO ..................................................................................................... 64

How Oke.io works? ............................................................................................................... 65

How much does Oke.io pay you? ......................................................................................... 65

Requirements and Restrictions: ........................................................................................... 66

Advertising Formats and Detailed Stats .............................................................................. 66

Payment Information ............................................................................................................ 66

## CONCLUSION .................................................................................................................. 67

# **CHAPTER ONE**

## **What is social media monetization?**

Social media monetization is effectively the process of generating revenue from your social media audience. This can be achieved in a number of different ways that we'll dive into in this post. Ultimately it will vary based on your product, the social channel you use, the technology available on each platform as well as the most vital ingredient – the level of insight you have on your audience. Knowing WHO you're speaking to and what their most common challenges, pain points, and desires are should not be underestimated.

When you know what your people want, you're in a much better position to tailor your product or service to their needs and make money from doing what you love. monetizing social media really is a win-win for everyone involved.

# Why you should monetize social media

With built-in audiences in the billions, social networks provide a great opportunity to connect with your target market. The value of using social media to drive brand awareness is undeniable. But, let's face it, social media can be time-consuming. You're always having to play by Facebook or Instagram's rules and maybe you're wondering whether all of the hours you spend posting, commenting, and interacting on these channels can really turn into solid sales for your product or service.

While it can sometimes feel disheartening to not get instant results, it's definitely possible to monetize social media. You're missing out on a huge opportunity to put more cash into your pocket if you're not capitalizing on the opportunities available. I mean, we've all heard of influencers on Instagram and YouTube who make millions by advertising their products and services – so that means it's highly achievable for you too.

# Defining your niche

If you want to monetize social media, it's important to know there's a fine line between spam and legit advertising. All too often people join affiliate programs, set up profile pages on Twitter and Facebook, and get down to work peddling their products to the masses. And then nothing happens. So, they decide to invest in paid advertising. Again, nothing happens. As the tumbleweed rolls across their profile pages, some may even be tempted to buy followers, which are either bots or not your ideal people.

Before you even think about how to monetize social media, you should think about your target audience. Rather than trying to be everything to everyone, you need to shift your thinking to a customer-centric approach. This is based on the simple reality that trying to reach as many people as possible in a world where we're so used to personalization and tons of competitors can look like you're taking a stab in the dark. You may have millions of followers, but it counts for nothing if none of them are genuinely engaged. It's better to have a few engaged users who get what you do and buy into it than having loads of fake or irrelevant followers who don't.

# Monetize-social-media

To build your community, you need to choose your niche wisely. Every brand needs a purpose choose a target demographic that aligns with that factor. It doesn't matter how small or specialized your niche is – there will be people out there who want to be a part of it, and social media provides the means to reach them. Once you've chosen your niche and defined your ideal customer, you'll be able to create content that speaks directly to their desires.

It's important to not get bogged down by vanity metrics or losing yourself in simply growing your followers. The reality is, you could have a thousand followers – but if they aren't your ideal client or customer and you're not speaking their language, then it won't mean much when you're trying to sell your product or service.

## Optimizing your social media profiles for monetization success

Before implementing our tips on monetizing social media, it's important to double-check that you have all of the basics in place first.

Things like ensuring your profile and cover photos are optimized with relevant images. Is it clear to your audience what you do? Does your cover photo have a phrase that sums up your service in a single sentence or are you using a random image that doesn't have much relevance? Does your profile or page have a history of strong content? By this, we mean how long ago did you last post any content – is it up-to-date? Does your content have any relevance to your audience? If your page is established this should be the case anyway, but if you're creating a new page or profile from scratch, we'd suggest waiting a few days to grow some content out around the page before attempting to grow it.

# **CHAPTER TWO**

## **How to monetize Tik-Tok**

Tik-Tok is the fastest growing social media platform in the world. The app has taken the social media world by storm. Since its release, it has been downloaded more than 1.5 billion times from the app store. There are currently over 800 million monthly active users on the platform.

With TikTok increasing in popularity, a lot of people are wondering if the platform can be monetized. Creators on the platform are asking if they can make money from their videos.

The simple answer is yes. Similar to other platforms like Instagram and YouTube, TikTok can be monetized. there are still several strategies you can use to make money on the platform.

Since the platform is still relatively new, there isn't a lot of competition yet. Many people are still trying to understand the viral video platform. That's why I have written this detailed guide to help you get started immediately.

If you are wondering how you can make money on TikTok, then you definitely want to read this book. Let's get started.

## Become a TikTok influencer

Similar to other popular social media platforms, one of the ways you can make money on TikTok is by becoming an influencer.

While it's no easy task becoming an influencer, it's definitely worth the effort. According to reports from Forbes, the most popular TikTok stars earned millions of dollars in the past year. Addison Rae with nearly 54 million followers was the highest-earning TikTok star. She generated an income of $5 million within a 12-month period. Charli D'Amelio (77 million followers) ranks 2nd with an estimated $4 million. Charli's sister ranks third, earning an estimated $2.9 million in the same time period.

The question, now, is – do you need millions of followers before you can become a TikTok influencer?

While the numbers matter, follower count is not the most important metric that brands use in choosing influencers to work with. Most brands look at the number of engaged followers. An influencer with 20,000 followers might have a more engaged audience than an influencer with 100,000 followers.

Another interesting fact is that most brands prefer to work with micro-influencers (influencers with a few hundred to 20,000 followers). While influencers with millions of followers can reach a larger number of people, they can be very expensive.

In summary, all you need to become an influencer is a few thousand engaged followers.

Next, let's see the steps you would need to take to become a TikTok influencer.

## Select your niche

It's important that you choose a niche that you are interested in. To become an influencer, you need to choose a niche that you can consistently create great content for. This will be difficult if you choose a niche that doesn't excite you or that you have no expertise in.

Find what you love doing and create amazing content around it. The only way you can attract an audience and get followers is by creating great content.

## Use a Pro account

TikTok offers the option of a pro account for both creators and businesses. The Creators account is best for public figures, artists, and influencers.

## Set up your profile

When setting up your profile, the two main areas to concentrate on are your profile picture and bio. These are the first things a user will see when deciding whether to follow you.

Your bio and profile picture should make a good first impression. If you feel like a picture is too bland, you can use a six-second video as your profile picture. This will add some personality to your profile.

## Understand your audience

Before you start creating videos for TikTok, try and understand your audience. To become an influencer, it's important that you create content that your target audience will love. Analyze the content that receives the most engagement. This will give you an idea of the kind of videos to create. You can also mirror the content strategy of other influencers in your niche.

## Create amazing content

The next step to becoming a TikTok influencer is creating amazing content. Quality content on TikTok sees a lot of engagement. The more creative and entertaining your videos are, the more likely they are to go viral. Viral videos tend to translate into new followers.

The following steps can help you create great TikTok content:
- Check out what your competitors are doing

- Take inspiration from the current trends
- Perform hashtag research to see what's trending in your niche
- Have some fun
- Be consistent

For increased visibility on TikTok, you need to post regularly and consistently. If you want to become an influencer, you need to upload quality content regularly. It's up to you to choose the frequency of your posts. Based on my personal research of popular TikTok influencers, 1 to 2 videos per day is great.

## Engage your audience

Once you start building a following, it's important that you engage with your audience. Interacting with your audience will help you reach influencer status faster. You can engage your audience by replying to their comments or asking them questions through your video captions.

## Declare that you are interested in brand collaborations

To start making money as an influencer on TikTok, you need to let brands know that you are interested in collaborating. You can let brands know this via your bio. You can also start an outreach campaign or join an influencer marketing agency to reach potential clients.

## Grow and sell TikTok accounts

Another way to make money on TikTok is by growing and selling TikTok accounts.

This is already popular on Instagram. Instagram users like 23-year-old Ramy Halloun makes $30,000 annually from flipping Instagram accounts.

This strategy can be replicated on TikTok.

To get started, find a niche and start creating interesting content around it. After growing the account to a certain level of followers and engagement, you can reach out to the brands in that industry and sell the TikTok profile to them.

The easiest kinds of accounts to sell are themed accounts. It's harder to sell personal accounts because they cannot be easily replicated by the new owners. With a themed account, you can easily find buyers. The followers of the profile are engaging with the account because of its theme. They might not even notice the change in ownership.

For example, if you create a TikTok account around videos of popular travel destinations and adventures, you can easily sell the profile to any business that offers travel services. You can also do this for other industries like fashion, food, fitness, beauty, etc.

The key is to create an account that has quality content. The more followers and better engagement rate the TikTok account has, the higher the price you can sell it for.

## Collect donations

You can make money on TikTok by collecting donations from your viewers on Livestream. TikTok allows creators to earn virtual gifts with monetary value via Livestream.

**Here is how it works:**

**Who can buy coins and gifts?**

Every user who is aged 18 or older can purchase gifts and coins from their profile. You can see the prices of the coins and gifts at the point of purchase. Once you have purchased the coins, they'll be credited to your account.

The prices of the coins also vary. You can get 100 coins for $1.39.

There are also different gifts you can purchase. You can use coins to purchase gifts. The most expensive gift is Drama Queen. It cost 5000 coins.

**What can users do with gifts?**

Gifts are used during a Livestream. TikTok users can offer gifts to their favorite creators to show their appreciation. They can contribute this gift by clicking the "Give Gift" button below the relevant User Content.

## What can content creators do with these gifts?

The gifts creators receive from their fans can be converted into diamonds. The creator can withdraw these diamonds in exchange for monetary compensation. The cash will be paid directly into PayPal or any other payment channel (if applicable).

Tip: Your first and last name on your profile must match your PayPal account before you can be paid. Your PayPal account must also be verified.

## There's a catch

Not every TikTok user is eligible to join TikTok's Livestream Program. Selected users are chosen at the discretion of the platform. If you want to qualify for the program, you can do the following:

- Consistently create quality content
- Increase your number of followers
- Increase the engagement rate, likes, comments, and shares you get on your videos.

The Chinese version of the app (Douyin) adds more monetization opportunities to the Livestream Program. Creators can add links to shopping carts on their Live videos. They can also hold auctions and people can buy products from them on Live.

Hopefully, these features will soon be added to the global version of the app.

## Run an influencer agency

You can make money on TikTok by managing influencers and influencer campaigns.

There are already a ton of influencer agencies for Instagram. You can do the same for TikTok.

Your influencer agency will help brands strategize, execute, and manage campaigns with TikTok influencers. Your agency will serve as a middle man between the influencers and brands looking for their services. You will help brands determine the best influencers to work with. You can take it a step further by creating a social marketing strategy to meet the brand's goals.

If you want to run an influencer agency, you should be able to do the following:

- Identify high performing TikTok influencers with a good track record
- You must be able to develop a relationship with top TikTok influencers
- You must have expertise in running successful social media and influencer marketing campaigns
- You must be able to create successful influencer campaigns for different advertising categories. This will help you diversify your income stream.

Note that TikTok already has its in-built internal influencer program. But it is a bit expensive. Smaller brands would probably prefer to work with influencer agencies because it would help them save money.

Starting a reputable influencer agency takes time and effort. To get ahead of the curve, it's important that you start your agency immediately. The best part is that you don't have to limit your services to just TikTok. You can also run influencer campaigns for other social media platforms.

## Become a TikTok consultant

If you are an expert on TikTok, there are a ton of brands and even individuals that would pay for your services.

If you know how to get thousands, even millions of views on your videos, you can teach others how to do the same for a consulting fee. Influencers can also offer consulting services. It's a good way to leverage your expertise and also diversify your income.

A good example of a TikTok consultant is Sean Young. He calls himself a professional TikTok consultant. He makes $10,000 a month advising celebrities and businesses on the best kind of content for their brands.

There's money to be made. So, if you really understand the platform and have a track record for creating viral videos with high engagement rates, you should start teaching others how to do so.

## Publish sponsored posts

You can make money on TikTok by publishing sponsored posts. According to business insider, you can make an average of $0.01 to $0.02 for each sponsored view on TikTok. So, if you have a video with 100,000 views, you can make 1000 dollars in sponsorships.

After you have built a following on the app, you can reach out to brands and offer your services. The best part is that you don't need to have millions of followers before you can pitch to brands. All you need are a few thousand engaged followers and you are good to go.

Look for brands that are interested in building their TikTok presence and reach out to them. You can also analyze the influencers in your industry to see the sponsors they work with. This will give you a good idea of brands to reach out to.

Once you have your list of target sponsors, send them a brief pitch in the form of an email. Here are the things to include in your pitch:

- Who you are?
- What you do?
- Important metrics like follower count and engagement rate
- What makes you an expert in that industry or niche?
- Your achievements. You can share success stories from your previous sponsorship campaigns.

Tip: When you are just starting out, it's a good idea to work with smaller brands first. This will help you build your portfolio.

## Sell your own merchandise

You can make money selling your own merchandise on TikTok. The best part is that you don't need thousands of followers before you can sell your own products or services.

Similar to other social media platforms, you can use TikTok to promote your business or store. The secret is creating engaging content that will attract the attention of your target customers. So even with 100 followers, you can start making sales via the platform.

For example, you may have a business selling beauty products. You can create creative 15-second makeup tutorial videos and post on TikTok. In the last 3 seconds of the video, you can add a promotional frame advertising your own products and how customers can reach you.

By putting up interesting and creative videos, you would attract attention to your TikTok profile and also generate leads for your business.

## How much money can you make from TikTok?

Influencers with up to 100k followers can earn between $500 and $2000 for sponsored posts in their videos. This value will also depend on the type of product, your number of followers, and engagement rate.

In fact, your engagement rate is one of the most important factors that determine how much you can earn on TikTok. Brands would like to see this figure before deciding if they will work with you and how much they will pay.

Influencers get paid more when they have a high engagement rate. Brands know that influencers can easily buy followers. Hence, engagement rate is a more genuine metric to analyze the value of an influencer.

This is the formula you will use in determining your engagement rate:

TikTok engagement rate = [(Number of hearts + number of comments)/number of followers] x100

## Does TikTok pay creators for videos?

TikTok is launching a $200 million fund to pay creators for their videos.

As TikTok grows, the company is trying to give creators an incentive to remain active on the platform. They don't want to make the same mistake that Vine did. Most Vine creators left the platform in favor of YouTube because they could monetize their YouTube videos. This led to the death of Vine.

The TikTok Creator Fund will directly pay creators for their videos. Although the company doesn't say how the payments will be made or how much each creator can earn.

What we do know is that you need to consistently post original, engaging videos that follow TikTok guidelines to qualify for the fund. A minimum number of followers is also required. The number isn't stated either. We will learn more about the fund soon. Creators in the United States can already apply for the fund as of August 2020.

Vanessa Pappas, the general manager of TikTok said this about the fund in a company blog post – "Through the TikTok Creator Fund, our creators will be able to realize additional earnings that reflect the time, care, and dedication they put into creatively connecting with an audience that's inspired by their ideas."

This fund will be another way for TikTok creators to earn money on the platform.

**Bonus: How to increase your TikTok views and boost your profile**

To really make money on TikTok, you need to significantly increase the number of video views you get on the platform. More views will translate into more followers and a higher engagement rate.

Along with the compulsory factor which is creating great content, here are other ways you can increase your TikTok views.

**Add hashtags to your videos**

Adding hashtags to your TikTok videos can help increase the visibility of your video. If you click on the Discover search tab, you will see a list of trending videos by hashtag.

For example, if you are creating a video for a viral challenge, you need to add the hashtag of the challenge to your video. When a TikTok user clicks on the hashtag link, your content would be one of the videos that show up. This will help increase the number of views you can get.

Tip: While it's great to add hashtags to your videos, avoid the generic ones. Look for specific hashtags in your niche so that your videos can easily stand out.

## Collaborate with other users

You can reach out to other users to collaborate on videos. By collaborating with other users, you increase your audience reach. If you partner with an influencer who has a huge following, you can significantly increase the number of views your videos get

## Post regularly

To increase the number of views your videos get and also your chances of getting to the 'For You' page, you should post videos regularly on the platform. A ton of videos are posted on the platform per minute. To avoid getting lost in a sea of content, you need to post videos regularly.

## Use TikTok effects in your videos

Use TikTok effects to help your videos stand out from the crowd. Under the Effects tab, you will find a wide range of effects that you can add to your videos. The effects are split into Trending, New, Interactive, Animal, Beauty, Funny, Editing, and World categories.

## tiktok effects trending 350@2x

Another effect I personally like is the green screen effect. This effect allows you to change the background of your videos. Use this effect to make your videos more entertaining.

## Use TikTok Ads

Brands that want to use TikTok to reach their target customers should consider using TikTok ads to amplify their reach. TikTok offers different advertising types that you can check out. To help you get started, we have written this in-depth guide to TikTok Ads.

Finally, TikTok is one of the fastest-growing social media platforms in the world. There are a ton of opportunities for making money on TikTok. From sponsored posts to selling your own merchandise on the platform. The key is to consistently create quality content that your followers will love and engage with.

This guide should help you get started with monetizing your videos on the platform.

# CHAPTER THREE

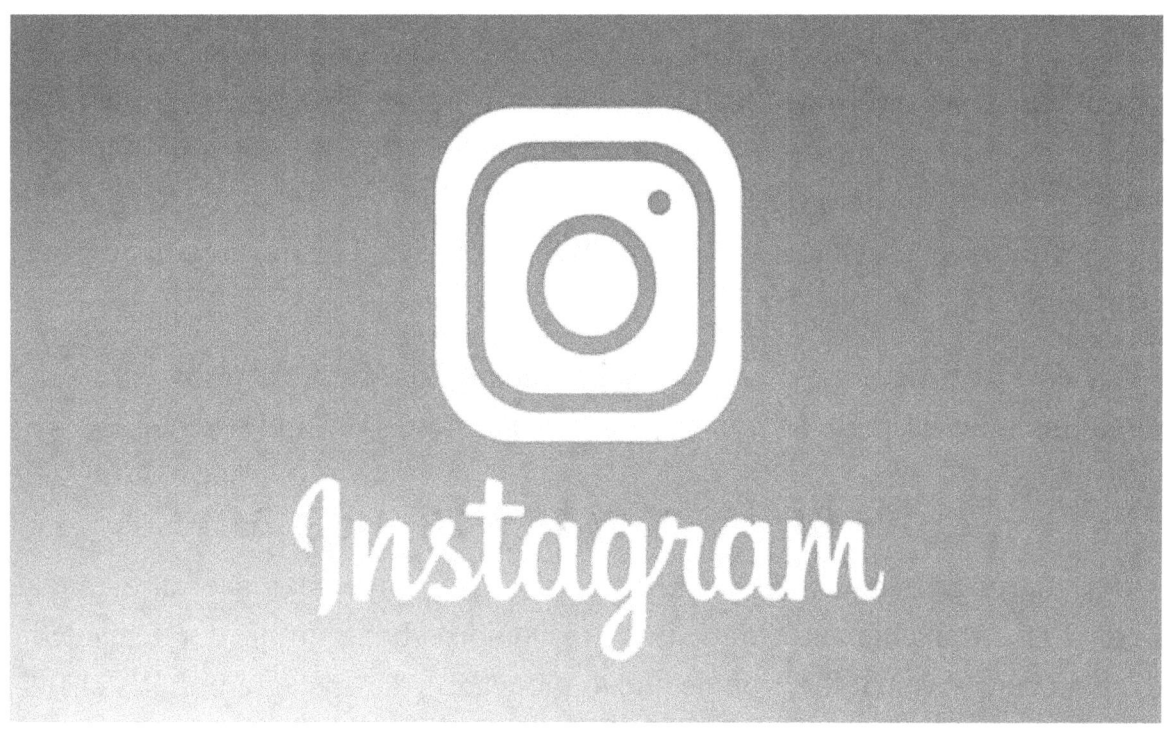

## How to Monetize Your Instagram

Instagram is more than just a fun place to post your holiday snaps. For many people, Instagram is a career. Thousands of influencers make millions of dollars every year on the platform – and you could too.

Nowadays Instagram became one of the most influential and active platforms with more than 1 billion registered users. Making money on Instagram and using it as a marketing platform for promoting products/services happened to be a new wave of digital marketing strategies. Instagram has passed the phase of being just a simple photo-sharing application, and now it is one of the best social media monetizing channels. Individuals and businesses started to monetize their Instagram accounts and made it an extraordinary source for getting income.

Next I am going to examine different aspects of how to grow an Instagram account, what steps are crucial to follow, and how to monetize Instagram using different platforms as well.

## Instagram in numbers

To get a wider understanding of an influential role Instagram plays, let's check some statistical information. Instagram is proven to be the second-most downloaded free mobile application (after YouTube), and this shows the continuous growth and attractiveness it has. The numbers are astonishing and there is no wonder why businesses are partially investing in their Instagram accounts as a part of SMM strategy

No doubt that it is possible to make money on Instagram by strategically promoting your business or yourself, generating more sales and revenue.

# How do I grow my Instagram?

Before starting to monetize your Instagram, you have to make sure that your account is sustainable and competitive. It would be better to have a dedicated and loyal audience even before you decide to monetize your Instagram. Let's check the main factors you have to take care of to build, grow, or improve your Instagram account.

## Correctly fill your BIO

Your BIO has to depict all the necessary information in a short way for customers to understand the core of your business/service. It is the first moment that catches customers' attention and inspires followers to catch up with your page.

Make sure that your name is your actual real name! It applies the same way if you are running a company's Instagram. Don't include lots of confusing numbers in your username, because it will just confuse the audience. People who are willing to find your Instagram account will search for your name and will type it in a clear way. Another point is that Instagram searching queries only display fields with your name and username in search results. It is essential to include the explanation of the main business/services you provide to your customers. Attach your webpage link or any other link you want people to click on. Besides, you can add the location. It can be just a city and country or the detailed physical location of your office.

## Post regularly

Your relationship with customers has to be effectively constructed. To do so, you need to regularly update your posts with new and interesting information. The statistics show that the more you post on Instagram, the faster your followers' rate will grow. Create your strategy for posts in advance: topics, pictures, descriptions. Keep posting during the most active time and "rush hours" for your followers. This will allow you to get more visibility since your post will appear just on the exact time your followers are online. Regular posts are connected to the engagement activity as well.

## Engagement

User engagement is one of the most important factors because it is genuine, creates brand loyalty, and draws attention.

The engagement should be a 2-way relationship and consist of mutual actions. You need to encourage the followers to spend time and be active on your Instagram profile. This is directly related to the content you produce. Another way is that you can get content inspiration from your audience. You can use different tactics by encouraging your audience to use your product. They can be featured on your profile or can receive a promo code after using your product/service. In addition to that, the audience has to know that you care about them, listen to them, and put your attention to their actions. Be active with the comment section by answering their questions, like back their photos or write a warm comment on their profile. This will help you to gain loyalty and being noticed.

## Video content

Instagram started as a photo-sharing platform, however, nowadays, the video content is taking over. Instagram allowed you to post a video up to 60 seconds, but the features are improving. Stories were introduced and a Carousel post (multiple images or video posts). These features enable a user to post multiple contents all together and give more options for video content to be published. Videos have a dazzling effect on user engagement and it is more interactive.

## Relevant hashtags

Instagram allows you to post up to 30 hashtags. Don't use random hashtags, but rather try to choose the most relevant and competitive ones. Competitive hashtags can be divided into 3 categories: low competitive (less than 12k existing posts), medium competitive (12k-100k existing posts), and highly competitive (more than 100k existing posts). Prepare your hashtags in advance, and try to use them from each category. This will give you an opportunity to be ranked higher with low competitive hashtags and to get a chance to achieve a bigger audience with highly competitive hashtags.

You can also create your personalized hashtag. Of course, it has to be related to your business activity. It can be your branded hashtag with the company name or a particular hashtag when you want your followers to be featured with your product/service.

## Establish connections with businesses and influencers

This external help from other known people from your niche will be beneficial for you to make your account grow faster. By establishing a connection with powerful Instagram account holders, you can achieve a win-win situation. There are a couple of ways to do so. The first one: you can agree to do a reciprocal promotion when you will post a photo/video mentioning another account, and in exchange, that account will do the same. Another way is that you agree on the one-time charge when you simply pay them to advertise you on their accounts. This is called a shoutout for a shoutout (S2S).

# Practical tactics to monetize your Instagram

You have to understand that easy to start making money on Instagram if you have an empty and fresh profile. You have to follow the steps, which we have mentioned above and grow your Instagram community. And now, it is time to analyze the ways you can monetize your Instagram account!

**1. Selling Shoutouts**

After creating a legit and competitive profile with a loyal audience, you can start making money on Instagram by selling shoutouts from your profile. In this way, you can simply give information to your audience using Stories and mentioning the business who contacted you for this purpose. But conditions might be different based on the agreement you came up with. The hardest part is that first, you have to grow your audience. Therefore, if you decide to start in this way, be professional and mention your contact details for future inquiries and collaborations.

## 2. Selling Instagram Accounts

It is another way of making money on Instagram. Many people are interested in buying an existing Instagram account with a lot of followers and then customizing it for their interests. There are 2 ways of implementing this strategy. The first one is when you are growing an account, getting more followers by yourself and then you sell it to someone, who is interested in this. The second method is that you buy an existing account for a low price and then resell it at a higher price. And that's the way to get a profit. But be aware of scammers who have more bot-followers that have a limited amount of time on Instagram.

## 3. Instagram Virtual Assistant

Lately, this particular way of monetizing Instagram became a trend. The idea behind it is that you will take care of all the necessary aspects of someone else's Instagram profile. A lot of small businesses and big companies are seeking to find a professional person, who will work on their Instagram page from scratch. The duties will be scheduling posts, create customized pictures, participate with followers on behalf of a company, making the entire page visually appealing, and many other detailed factors. Usually, it considered to be a remote work, but the reports on the activity and engagement have to be tracked.

## 4. Sponsored (Promoted) posts

This tactic will work really well for you if you already have a lot of followers and became an influencer. Usually, this kind of posts includes #sponsored or #ad hashtags. In this tactic, you are making money on Instagram by promoting branded products/services on the agreed conditions. This way is more profitable than shoutouts because based on the number of followers you have; you can charge a higher price for brands. In 2017, Instagram has launched a new option, which is "Paid Partnership". It allows an influencer to tag the company at the top of the post (instead of the location feature). This feature brings more transparency to the post and helps businesses track how their promotion is performing.

## 5. Sell your photos

Stock photos were important before and will be demanded in the future as well. The photography niche has a high demand and high competition as well. Don't expect to find customers immediately and get paid with a reasonable amount in the beginning. However, Instagram is an amazing platform to promote and advertise your photos and get featured and noticed by other users. Above all, to get a sustainable competitive advantage you have to be selective, creative, and unique with your photographs.

## 6. Sell your own product/service

If you already have an existing business, you definitely have to create a business account on Instagram and other social media platforms. By having a personal Instagram account, you can mention in your BIO the information about your business account and its activity. In addition, there is a good chance that your existing followers will visit your business account and will be more likely to purchase your product/service.

## 7. Monetize your own experience and hobbies

Your own experience and hobbies can be a driving force to create an Instagram account and stand in the chosen niche. Let's say you are a traveler or your hobby is knitting. By showing and explaining everything from your own experience, you will establish an audience of people who have the same interests. Later on, your hobbies can become a perfect source of income with the help of Instagram. In this way, there is a huge chance for you to become an influencer in a chosen niche, which later will drive more money opportunities for you.

## 8. Affiliate marketing

This is one of the most famous ways if you want to monetize your Instagram. In this particular way, you become a representative or an "ambassador" of a company.

As a result, your income will be related to the number of products that were sold through your Instagram page. The commission varies from 10% up to 80% from each product sold. Usually, you will be given a special link or promo code you have to mention or post (generally your name will be included in the link or promo code to make it easier to track sales), and the percentage of discount users that have used this respective link or promo code.

# Monetize your Instagram with different tactics and platforms

Let's discover what platforms you can use to monetize your Instagram. These platforms are divided into different Instagram tactics depending on your choice and interests.

## For Affiliate Marketing:

Clickbank: This platform has a variety of products to promote in different niches. It shows you detailed information on commission, an average price per sale, sale statistics, and a company's information.

ShareASale: Provides an option for sign up both for affiliate representatives and merchants. Products are represented across 40 different categories. Also, you will be able to track promotions on social media.

## For Selling Photographs:

Twenty20: This famous marketplace allows you to sell your photographs with a wide range of customers and companies all around the world. You will keep your rights for a photo and you can resell it a few times. It is possible to sell your photo at a price of 2$ or participate in photo challenges with high competition, but also the reward will be higher.

Snapwire: The platform with authentic custom photos. In the beginning, you have to upload as many high-quality photos as possible. To be easily discovered by brands, you have to use the right hashtags. You will have an option to either sell your photos directly via Snapwire platform or upload photos that match brands' request. "Recently purchased" option allows you to see what photos were recently sold and get some motivation.

## For Influencers:

Buzzoole: An influencer platform, which allows you to search for brands that match your niche. There is a dashboard in your profile where you can see the analysis of your page with what topics are more suitable for your profile.

Tapinfluence: This platform is unique in its approach. Instead of you searching for brands and post opportunities, brands will show their interest in working with you and you will be notified. You can choose multiple topics and subtopics to include in your dashboard. Other information as total reach, cost per engagement, location, and rating position is also displayed in a convenient way.

Tribe: Is considered to be the fastest-growing branded marketplace platform. It connects creative agents and influencers. The price will be directly related to the number of followers you have. The minimum number of followers are required to have is 3K with the minimum rate per post 75$. There is no exact maximum price, but it is mentioned to be more than 1200$ per post.

**For Shoutouts:** One of the most famous platforms that connect you with the top influencers with a large audience of followers. Some of the influencers are famous actors and singers. The influencers' information is easily accessible and transparent, you can immediately see what price are they charging, how many followers they have, and their Instagram name. Prices are starting at 5$ and could reach more than a few hundred dollars.

**BuySellShoutouts:** The platform offers different services like shoutouts, likes, mentions, organic growth service, followers, and others. These services are available for 2 platforms, which are Instagram and Facebook. If you have more than 50K followers, you can become a partner with this company and start selling your shoutouts.

**For Selling Accounts**: This company is cooperating with more than 2000 companies who are ready to buy or sell influence accounts. Has 4 different type of payment, so it gives more option for money transactions. Besides buying/selling

Instagram accounts, it also gives the same option for Facebook, Twitter, Tumblr, and YouTube pages.

**FameSwap**: One of the leading platforms, which provides offers to buy and sell not only Instagram accounts, but also YouTube and Tiktok accounts. You can easily find the information on the selling price, the number of followers, and when the offer was added to the website. It provides safely encrypted transactions and 24/7 post-purchase support.

# CHAPTER FOUR

## How to Make Money on Facebook

Everybody uses Facebook. Okay, slight exaggeration. But with over two billion users worldwide, including more than 214 million in the United States alone, it is very, very widespread.

It's revolutionized news, culture, social interaction, and more. But it's not just a way for you to keep in touch with old high school friends, share your funny dog photos, or post videos from your beach vacation.

And the reality is that no matter what business or market you are in, chances are you can reach a segment of your audience on Facebook.

Facebook is also a powerful money-making platform. In fact, there are many ways you could potentially make money on Facebook. Let's take a look at the various ways you can use Facebook to market, advertise, and promote your business - or just make some money on the side.

## 1. The Facebook Marketplace

This is one of the simplest ways to make money on Facebook. Essentially, Facebook allows you to sell items on a special section Marketplace " of the site. Many towns, cities, and communities have set up buy/sell pages or you can simply search by geographic location, product name, or category. That way buyers can quickly see a wide range of choices in the surrounding area.

You can post used or new items to sell, everything from laptops to cell phones to cars to furniture. It's like Craigslist on steroids. Here are some tips when it comes to selling on the Facebook Marketplace:

- Make sure to include clear pictures of what you're selling.
- Provide details like model number, condition (be honest), etc.
- Make sure you are selling it for the right price. Check what the same or similar items are selling for from other Marketplace sellers or on other sites like eBay or Craigslist.
- Keep in mind there is some negotiation with potential buyers and many will try to low-ball you. If you don't think it's a fair price, you're under no obligation to take the offer.
- Chances are you're not going to create a full-time business buying or selling items on Facebook, but this is a quick way to make some extra cash. If you're already selling items on eBay or Craigslist this is another avenue for you to reach more people and expand your potential audience of buyers.

## 2. Facebook as a Traffic Driver

The great thing about Facebook is that its algorithms examine where you go online, what you click on the site, what videos you watch, etc. Then it brings more of those types of posts to your attention. Facebook is also, of course, a way to connect like-minded people, organizations, and companies.

You can take advantage of this to make money on Facebook. You'll do it not by selling to people directly on the platform as with the Marketplace but rather compelling people to click on links on your Facebook page that takes them to your e-commerce site, landing page, or other website connected to your online business.

This is often referred to as two-step marketing. You're not trying to make a sale on Facebook (because people generally aren't there to buy), rather you're trying to get their attention and interest and get them off of Facebook clicking over to your website.

There you can sell them products or ask them to sign up to your email list (we'll cover that in depth in the next section). This Facebook traffic is very qualified—these are people interested in your product offers. When you run ads on Facebook you can target by demographics, interests, and even people who have already expressed interest in your product, business, and brand so the traffic is very qualified.

To boost your traffic, you need to post regularly to your Facebook page. You can post sales pitches, product launches, and other related things to your business. Strong copy and compelling offers can bring in a lot of traffic. But you should also have useful content on your page that engages the prospect—that's what'll keep them coming back. You could post industry news, funny stories, etc. Photos and videos are very important these days—people want to watch them. And they don't have to be professionally produced.

If you have a blog, you should also post a link to every new post on your Facebook page. Same with any new YouTube videos or any other content you post elsewhere online. It's all about driving as much traffic as possible. You may even consider paying for ads just to have people see your free content and go back to your website as well. This way you can build a retargeting audience and run ads to them in the future.

The idea is to include content that gets people to like your Facebook page, so it shows up in their news feed and they send it to friends too.

### 3. Using Facebook to Generate Leads

This goes right along with #2 but we wanted to focus on this way to make money on Facebook because it's very effective, although it is more of gradual way to earn income.

Basically, all the Facebook users out there are potential leads for your business. Not everybody, of course, just those folks who are interested in your products. The cool thing is that Facebook makes it easy to find these folks… and for them to find you. Again, you need a Facebook page for your business.

Include useful content to engage the users. Also include links to your website or a landing page asking them to sign up to your list to get a newsletter or updates, as well as special offers. It's important that you give them some incentive for signing up, like a free eBook or special report related to your niche.

With Facebook you can also include an email opt-in form directly on your Facebook page.

You should also go to fan pages or Facebook groups that are in the same industry or niche and start posting—this networking can bring more people to your page or directly to your website or landing page.

Once these people are on your email list you can continue to send them offers, as well as useful content like a newsletter. This is a great way to warm them up to the idea of buying from you. And you can offer them increasingly more expensive products over time as they buy the lower cost products first and then are ready for higher ticket items.

Another strategy that is working well is to post links that simply go to content pieces or blog posts on your website. You're simply running ads to good □uality content you've created. Once they arrive to your content, there you can offer a content upgrade by way of getting onto your email list. This is a less direct method but can make your ads more cost effective.

## 4. Facebook Ads

The old saying goes, "You have to spend money to make money." And that's certainly the case with running paid ads on Facebook. You've seen these ads, they're the little banners on the right side of the page, as well as the sponsored posts that show up directly in the news feed.

Again, cookies that follow you around online, follow you to Facebook. So that ads that appear are something you might be interested in and you're more likely to click and even buy the product. When you're an advertiser that's great news because your ads are getting in front of the eyeballs of the right people.

One note of caution. Like any type of online advertising, Facebook ads can be pricey and it's quite easy to spend a lot of money with no return if you don't know what you're doing.

So, before you use this method to make money on Facebook, you should have all your systems in place, you should have been in business for a while, and you should have some cash in reserve because there will be some trial and error before you find ad copy and an offer that works. You should also have good tracking in place so you know exactly which ads are working and which ones are not; that way you're not wasting money on ads that don't work and can pump more money into the ads that are working.

A related method to this is boosting posts. When you find a post on Facebook that is working well and engaging your prospects, you can "boost" it by paying some extra money. Boosting puts it in front of more people.

Boosting posts is the simplest way to do a Facebook ad; once you find a boost post that works well you should use Facebook's more advanced ad options to promote those posts that do well.

## 5. Bringing Customers to Your Bricks-and-Mortar Business

Customers expect every business they interact with to have a Facebook page. This includes businesses with physical locations like shops, retail stores, restaurants, and more. So, it's important that you have a Facebook page that clearly shows your location, what your place is all about, what products or services you offer, etc.

You can also include news of sales and discount offers or special events. For example, you can post about the weekly happy hour at your restaurant. And if somebody posts a question or comment – be sure to respond in a timely manner. Get a conversation going with your fans.

The goal here is to have people like your page so your new posts are in their newsfeed. Then when they see a special offer they like, they come in to your physical location. You want to keep your place of business top of mind with your prospects so they come visit you.

Admittedly this strategy only really works if you have a physical business, but it's worth mentioning here. Also, you should encourage all of your customers to like your page and have them follow you on Facebook for news, specials, coupons, and updates. A simple sign at the register encouraging people to follow you on Facebook can work or you may even incentivize people to follow you by offering something.

Another important note: you can only run paid ads to a business page; not your personal profile.

## 6. Sell Affiliate Products

Affiliate marketing is one of the quickest ways to get started doing business online. And the cool thing is that Facebook is a great way to get into this type of venture. It makes it so easy.

The basic model works like this:

- You sign up for an affiliate program. There are dozens out there but a great place to start is Click Bank, CJ Affiliate, and Amazon.
- You promote products from those sites on a Facebook page catered all around a specific hot niche.
- Whenever somebody clicks on the link and buys the product, you get a commission – generally from 20 percent to 80 percent.

As with any strategy to make money on Facebook, it's important to post regularly and engage with your audience. That creates trust and makes more likely people will buy. Also, be sure to track those numbers so you know which campaigns are working and which ones are not.

There are many ways to profit from spending time and effort on Facebook. It's one of the most versatile platforms for making money online. Try one or several of these methods to see which one works best for you. Best of luck.

# Make Money with Your Twitter Account

There are several ways that you can make money through the social network without trying to sell your own products or services.

Twitter is a powerful platform unto itself, not just a conduit for marketing another site. You can create a Twitter account around a profitable niche — making money online, online education, or motherhood, for example — and amass a large number of followers interested in that niche. Then you can tweet links to interesting content from around the web, offering your followers something of value without ever having to create content yourself.

So how do you make money? The same way you do on a blog: Selling advertising, sponsored links, and affiliate marketing. Here are a few programs that can help you make money on Twitter:

Tip: To make money on Twitter, you would also need an efficient way to publish, schedule, monitor, listen, comment, and so on. You can use Agorapulse to maximize all these in less time.

## 1. Sponsored Tweets

Sponsored Tweets is a well-known ad service for Twitter it allows you to set your own price-per-click for ads that you tweet. You can choose the ads you tweet from a list of available ads that are updated regularly. You must have at least 50 followers, 100 tweets, and an account that is at least 60 days old to sign up for this service.

## 2. MyLikes

MyLkes is an extensive ad platform can be used on Twitter, Tumblr, YouTube, and your blog. You get to choose ads from thousands of advertisers, and you get to schedule the time the advertisement will be tweeted from your account. You can earn as much as $0.42 per click, and you can get a payout weekly.

## 3. Ad.ly

Ad.ly is another ad service that lets you send out advertisements in your tweets. However, you don't get paid-per-click. Instead, you create a profile of your interests, then advertisers can choose your account to publicize a campaign. You agree to send out a specific number of tweets on a specific schedule, and you get paid a lump sum.

## 4. Rev Twt

Rev Twt is a Twitter-based advertising service and is a pay-per-click platform. The more followers you have and the higher reputation you have, the greater access you will have to higher-paying campaigns. Payout is made via PayPal when you have reached $20 in earnings.

## 5. Twittad

The Twittad platform claims to be one of the first sponsored-tweet networks. You are able to set your own cost-per-click, but you have to wait for advertisers to accept your bid. You will also have to identify your niche so that advertisers can match their products with you appropriately. Payment is made via PayPal when you have reached $30 in earnings.

There are many other ways you can make money with your Twitter account, including selling banner ads on your profile page, setting your own rates and selling direct sponsored tweets, charging to send a personal message to your followers, or charging for access to your private list of followers. These advertising services can also help you make money through pay-per-click advertising, which can be especially lucrative if you have a large following.

# CHAPTER FIVE

## How To Monetize Your WordPress Website

If you want to make money from your WordPress website either as a blogger or as a regular website user and don't know what to do, this section is for you.

I get tons of emails and DMs almost every day from friends and colleagues asking me how they can optimize their WordPress websites and make a lot of money. The thing is, making money from your website is both technical and easy to learn.

There are thousands of WordPress websites available on the internet that are either making money from their websites or are not. For users who wish to make money from their websites, it then means they have to do more than having a WordPress site to stand out from the pack.

In this section, you will learn what WordPress is, why monetizing your website or blog is important and how to monetize your WordPress website.

## What is WordPress?

WordPress is the most used, easiest to use and most powerful blogging and website content management system (CMS) designed with PHP and MySQL in existence today.

WordPress is dated back to 2003 and started as a joint effort between Matt Mullenweg and Mike Little. It is widely reported that Christine Selleck Tremoulet, a friend of Mullenweg, suggested the name "WordPress".

WordPress allows users to create and publish content for different purposes. It also allows users to select themes from pre-installed resources that are either free or paid for. With WordPress, you can also install plugins that help you achieve more functionality for your website.

## WordPress.com vs WordPress.org

WordPress.com was created by the co-founder of WordPress, Matt Mullenweg. Because of the same founder, many users confuse WordPress.com with the popular WordPress.org software.

WordPress.com comes with a free limited plan and a number of paid plans. WordPress.org, on the other hand, "the real WordPress", as is popularly called, is the platform that we all know about. It is open source and 100% free for any user to use. All that is needed is a domain name and web hosting with reliable web hosting services. This is why it is also referred to as self-hosted WordPress.

## What You Need to Monetize Your Website

A WordPress Account: Creating a WordPress account is easy and free. It is, however, more profitable to create a paid WordPress website that comes with added features and functionalities that allow making money form the web easy. Simply sign up for an account with your email address and password on www.wordpress.com.

A Domain Name: It goes to assume that you have decided what you intend to do with your WordPress website. Your domain name should advisably reflect your website niche, the industry you belong to, and should be hosted on reliable hosting platforms.

WordPress themes: WordPress themes give you amazing CSS designs that beautify your website and can keep your visitor coming.

Plugins: A plugin, add-on or extension is any software component that adds a specific feature to an existing computer program. Plug-ins help to enable customization.

# Why you need to Make Money from Your Website

It is possible: Making money off your website is not an impossible task. It is daunting, no doubt, but with dedication and commitment, you can set up your website to become a money-making machine.

It is profitable: Not only is making money from your website possible, but it is also very profitable. As you would soon see, many strategies and methods abound that would help you get the most profit out of your website.

It is valuable: Making money from your website is one thing, but making your website valuable is another thing. The logic here is that the more valuable your website is, the more monetized it can get and also, the more monetized your website is, the more valuable it gets. In other words, a money-making website brings you more visitors, readers, followers and community engagement.

# How to Make Money on WordPress: The Strategies

Yayyyy! You got to this stage of the book. Now that you're here, it means you understand what WordPress is, what monetizing a WordPress website is, what you need to get started on WordPress, and why monetizing a website should be important to you.

Let's dig into some strategies that you can adopt to make money on your existing or intending WordPress website.

## How to Make Money from Affiliate Marketing

Affiliate marketing is probably the most popular strategy to help you cash out and monetize your website. With Affiliate marketing, you can net as much as $10 to $100 from a single sale. It involves recommending a product or service to your audience using custom tracking links, and then get a referral commission for every time someone buys using your link.

As many product and service companies both home and abroad offer affiliate programmes, there exist tons of affiliate programmes available online that you can sign up for with an almost endless number of niches for you to choose.

The caveat, however, is that you need to be smart about this strategy so you don't "overpromote" and come across as being too selly.

These sites and brands have some of the most profitable affiliate programmes that would benefit you.

- Amazon Associates
- ShareASale
- SEMRush

Here's how you get started. Once you have selected any of option above, you can register with any of them. After registration, you would have a dashboard and a custom affiliate link you can promote and advertise by putting on your website, social networking sites or email campaigns.

Afterwards, head on to your website to install a WordPress plugin like ThirstyAffiliates that will help you manage your affiliate links. This plugin allows you to quickly insert links into posts and sidebar content, create custom links, and track how your links are performing on your site.

Thereafter, you need to optimize and promote your links via as many content marketing channels as possible in order to get people to buy products using your custom links. Once a purchase is made using your link, you automatically get paid a commission by your affiliate company.

Affiliate marketing is not as difficult as people deem it to be if only you understand the processes. It is also stress-free, as you do not need to buy or create any product. All you need is your marketing channel and your promotional skills.

## How to Make Money with Google Adsense

Yes, Google Adsense has a lot of money making opportunities. This is arguably one of the top web monetization strategies out there.

Google Adsense is a "Cost per click" advertising platform and a very easy way to make money from your blog. It lets you as a Publisher display ad from Google on your website. By displaying these CPC ads with Google Adsense, you receive a certain amount of money each time an ad on your website is clicked by a visitor.

With Google Adsense, cost per click is set by the advertiser. Here's the best part. Google Adsense is stress-free. You don't have to deal with advertisers or worry yourself about collecting money. Google transacts with the advertisers to set advert rates and determines which publishers (you) have enough website traffic to display the ads.

To get started, apply to become a Publisher on Google Adsense with your Gmail account. Once set up, login to your Google Adsense account to get the ad codes to place on your website.

From experience, ads in post/content and header sections generate more clicks because they're more strategically positioned than other sections like the sidebar.

Once the codes have been added, Adsense would begin to display ads at your specified locations and according to your niche within a couple of hours.

The catch, however, is that you need to make your website generate high traffic levels so that you can make substantial revenue from the ads that you display.

You should also be cautious about clicking on your own ads. Asides being insubstantial, that can get you banned from the platform. It will serve you well to read and understand the terms and conditions of use.

## How to Make Money from Content Creation

Selling you're own products (digital, especially) on your website is probably the most "commonsensical" thing to do to make money from your website.

I mean, why else would you have a website if you do not wish to monetize it by selling your products via the website? Website owners and bloggers are usually known for selling digital products like e-books, plugins, themes, pictures, online courses, how-to guides, webinar hangouts, softwares, fonts and other graphics, etc.

Others even provide services like dieting consultation, coaching, fitness and wellbeing consulting or you can even open an e-commerce store with WooCommerce. The idea is to sell a product or service that represents your website niche.

## How to Make Money from Product Reviews

Whether you're writing a sponsored post for a hosting company you use and enjoy, or writing paid reviews for a brand on your website, you can also make money by writing product reviews on your site.

Writing reviews with affiliated links is one particularly profitable way that review writing can be. You basically need to try out products related to your niche for free, get an affiliate link, and then insert the link in the review post to get your readers clicking.

You can use PayPerPost and SponsoredReviews to connect you with businesses who may be interested in paying you for review posts. The options are interesting because with this strategy, you can make as much as $100 from just one post.

Best practice would be to always write honestly objectively about the product. While you obviously need to write positively about the product, there are ways that you can sound more rational and less opportunistic.

## How to Make Money from Display Ads

One good way to also monetize your blog is by putting up display ads on your website. Display ads are also a very popular monetization strategy. To get interested advertisers, you can contact some big brands to pitch your website value to them and get them to hire you as a publisher of their ad on your website.

While Google Adsense randomizes and places ads on your site without your pick, display ads put you in control. They involve you selecting which ad is put on your site. All you need to do is determine your ad rates by yourself, and place the ads that you get.

To get started, you need to gain enough visits and followers on your blog, that way, you can negotiate higher ad rates.

You should now know that your website is a money-making machine and you should now have a basic understanding of how you can achieve this. As you must have read, you definitely do not need to be a geek in WordPress to make a living. The above strategies are quite self-actionable and can be implemented by anyone who is tech-savvy and able to manage a blog.

Rest assured, earnings may start slowly, but as you work consistently, your earnings will consistently increase.

# CHAPTER SIX

## How To Monetize Your LinkedIn Account

Think LinkedIn is just for connections? Think again. The popular social network has many opportunities for monetization, especially for people who already have an established business or brand. If you haven't tried any of these LinkedIn techniques, you may actually be leaving money on the table. It's time to update your profile, flesh out your brand story, and start making connections. How does LinkedIn make money for you? Read on to find out!

## Requirements for monetization

**1. Build up your LinkedIn profile:** You can't go straight from "basic LinkedIn profile" to "money-making machine." Baby steps. First, you need to make your LinkedIn profile as complete as possible, including adding a recent, good-looking picture and filling out the all-important professional portfolio section. A resume tells people what you've done; a portfolio proves it. Once you have this done, remember to:

Post every morning…at least. If you need to, use HootSuite to schedule an entire week's worth of posts in advance.

**2. Tell a Brand Story**: Your LinkedIn profile can't look like you'd be willing to accept any old job or opportunity. You need to clearly create a brand story — a mission for yourself or your business. You aren't waiting for your career to happen; you're already off and running, halfway to achieving a specific goal.

Add your LinkedIn badge to your company website, wherever you describe your core mission. Also, be sure to feature any LI customer reviews you get.

**3. Form relationships:** I know you've probably ignored a lot of those "Invitation to connect on LinkedIn" emails. You've probably also ignored the "So and so's new job" emails. Time to dig into your email archives and start responding. The more connections you have, and the more you interact with those connections, the stronger your LinkedIn network becomes. It's also important to write and solicit recommendations — not just the "endorsed skills" type, but the actual written recommendations that appear on your profile. These helps prove that you are trustworthy and that you have strong relationships with former and current colleagues.

Create LinkedIn groups where you can engage your target market, study and participate in their interactions to see what kinds of topics are drawing engagement. Address these topics in your company stream.

Upload many relevant files on a regular basis (not just pictures from time to time–pdfs, videos, and infographics every day) and keep it organized.

Ask questions and hold contests using Targeted posts for select audiences.

# Earning from LinkedIn

Leverage your saleable product or service: There are many ways to make money on LinkedIn, but the first and easiest way is often to create a saleable product. Many people choose to monetize information products, such as motivational guides to success in their chosen fields or how-to technical manuals for their areas of expertise. Information products are great money generators because they are nearly always digital (ebooks, PDFs, etc.), meaning that they do not cost much money to manufacture or ship. Other saleable products include hardcopy books as well as products related directly to your business. If you sell bespoke shoes, for example, make sure people can buy your product by clicking to your store from your LinkedIn profile.

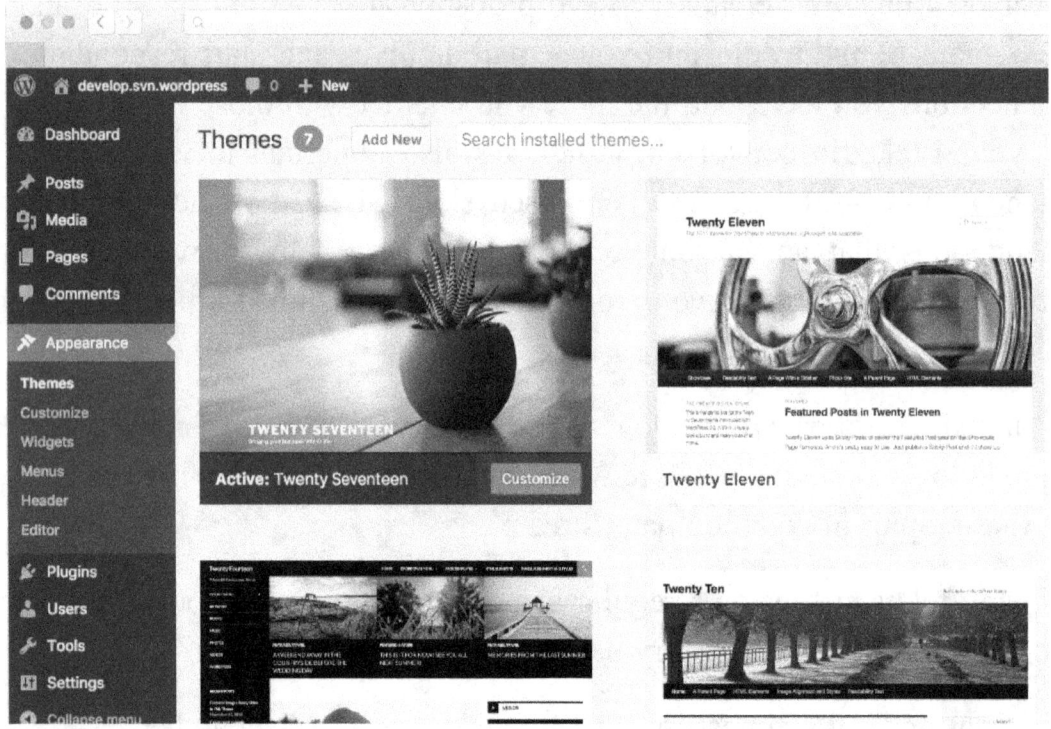

**Offer consulting services**: If you have expertise in a specific area, make sure your LinkedIn connections know that you offer consulting services. Many people make plenty of extra money every month by talking to other businesses or entrepreneurs about what they've learned. If you go the consultant route, make sure it is fully integrated into your brand — you don't want anyone to think you're hustling for consultant jobs simply because you need a little extra cash.

Again, targeting specific audiences with Recommendation Ads are the best way to increase engagement.

**Promote Affiliate Products**: Affiliate marketing is a stable way of generating money online in general. Essentially, it consists of advertising or promoting another company's product or service in exchange for a percentage of the sales that result from your recommendation.

Go into your groups and answer some of the questions there with relevant affiliate marketing review posts.

Post your affiliate posts in your Publications section too, as well as sending it to your email list.

# CHAPTER SEVEN

## How to Make Money on Twitch

The most significant change in social media usage over the last couple of years has been an immense increase in the number of videos shared and consumed. While the bulk of that has involved people sharing videos on platforms such as YouTube and Facebook, there has also been a considerable upsurge in live streaming.

One niche that attracts relatively tech-savvy supporters is gaming. So, it should be of little surprise that gamers have taken to live streaming more ⬜uickly than most other genres. Twitch is the streaming platform of choice for gamers.

It doesn't take long for influencers to sprout up on a platform, and as we have seen in Top 20 Twitch Influencers (Streamers) Every Gamer Should Follow, these including many of the gamers who release top "gaming highlight" videos on YouTube. Many of these gaming influencers earn their incomes from a mix of

Twitch Streaming, their YouTube videos, and in some cases, professional game playing.

These gaming broadcasters have discovered how to make money on Twitch. It can be a lucrative platform for influential and entertaining gamers. There is also a small percentage of successful Twitch broadcasters who have managed to build a following in non-gaming niches.

Some well-known gamers have clearly found the formula to make good money on Twitch. Shroud, for instance, takes in more than $100,000 a month from subscribers alone. And this is just from one source of income. Once you add in sponsorship and other money-making techniques, the top Twitch influencers are generating impressive earnings.

Obviously, few everyday Twitch users will have a large enough support base to make money on Twitch. Most don't have any intention of doing so. They merely spend time on the platform watching their favourite broadcasters and influencers playing and commentating on their play.

If you have a realistic aim to make money, you need to begin by meeting the criteria to become a Twitch Affiliate. If you are serious about building up a Twitch-based income, you should then work on reaching the level of support where Twitch will offer you an opportunity to become a Partner.

Everyday users need to work on improving their streaming skills and building up a following before they should consider making money on Twitch.

The following ways to make money on Twitch are theoretically open to any Twitch user. These are mainly "off platform" methods of making money, not officially connected to the Twitch platform itself.

## Affiliate Links

A common way people earn money online is to join various affiliate programs. This is different from the Twitch Affiliate Program.

Affiliate marketing involves marketing other people's' products online, using a customized link to a site where potential customers can buy the product. If they follow your link and make a purchase, you receive a percentage of the money they spend.

Many Twitch streamers sign up to some affiliate network that sells products that interest gamers. If somebody follows an affiliate link from a streamer's Twitch page and buys something, then the broadcaster will receive a percentage of the money the person spends on that company's website.

## Search for Amazon Products to Affiliate

Amazon has the best-known affiliate program in the world. Amazon owns Twitch, so it makes it particularly easy for Twitch streamers to work as an Amazon affiliate. Amazon calls the affiliate program, Gear on Amazon. Streamers can showcase Amazon products in a widget on their page. Any fans who click on the widget are redirected to the relevant Amazon sales page for the product. The broadcaster receives a percentage of any sales revenue earned during the visit.

Of course, you don't want to lose credibility with your audience. This means that it makes sense that you limit your affiliate advertising to products you use and recommend yourself. Likewise, don't offer links to competing products. Decide which competing product you like and link to that one. You shouldn't, for instance, hedge your bets by providing affiliate links to both Coca-Cola and Pepsi.

## Selling Customized Merchandise

This is another income source that is not directly related to Twitch itself. Hence it is available to any Twitch broadcaster. Of course, if you don't have a large following, you are unlikely to have many people wanting to spend money on buying a mug or tee-shirt featuring the face of a "nobody" they have never heard of. But once you have made a name for yourself on Twitch, your fans will be prepared to pay for your customized merchandise.

The easiest way to do this is to set up an online store and then place a link to it on your Twitch page. You can then promote it in your feed and direct your fans to your online store. Many short-run manufacturers are happy to create customized "fanboy" merchandise you could sell.

## Donations

You can ask your followers for donations to help you spend more time entertaining them on Twitch. Although Twitch has a type of mini donations called Bits, you have to be an Affiliate or Partner to have access to these. We look at Bits in more detail below.

You could make a direct request for donations on your page. To do this, you will first need to set up a link using PayPal, Stripe or some other online payment processing system. You would then make donation requests in your stream, giving the PayPal or other payment details. You could set up a donations goal and show your progress towards the goal. This acts as an incentive for your fans to help you.

We have previously discussed how you can use Twitch Alerts to provide a graphical stimulus to encourage people to make donations to you.

It may be simpler to collect donations through a third party website, such as Patreon. You would need to go to the Patreon website first and create a profile. You would then link to your Patreon profile from Twitch, along with your social media accounts.

One word of warning, however. There have been quite a few cases where scammers have made fake donations. They make their donation, but later file a chargeback, leading to the streamer losing the donation. So before you celebrate that "larger-than-life" donation make sure that you see the cash first.

## Sponsorship

Twitch is the live streaming site of choice for gamers and enjoys many keen, enthusiastic viewers in the genre. They tend to stay on-site for much longer than other social platforms, and often follow their preferred streamers with a passion. This makes it an ideal online venue for brands to target gamers.

If a brand feels they have a natural affinity with a particular streamer's audience, then it makes sense for them to sponsor the streamer on Twitch and engage in influencer marketing.

Any company that sells a product to "gamer-type people" can benefit from Twitch sponsorship. As well as the gaming companies themselves, this includes companies selling computers, gaming consoles, phones, accessories, website hosting, food, drinks, takeaways, fashion, music and more niches.

As sponsorship deals are made outside of Twitch, it does not matter whether a streamer is a Partner or Affiliate. Of course, like all influencer marketing, brands will typically choose to work with broadcasters who influence their followers' decision making. So it would be atypical for a small broadcaster on Twitch, who has not yet reached Affiliate status, to receive sponsorship.

## Tournament Winnings

If you are a good player, one way you can earn money while streaming on Twitch is by entering a tournament and winning (either by yourself or in a team, depending on the game).

In reality, this option will generally be restricted to professional gamers, or people in pro teams, as it will be to difficult for average gamers to beat them.

Smaller players may be able to join tournaments on ESL or with GameBattles by MLG and earn some money – broadcasting your battles for your Twitch fans as you play, of course.

Income Sources Available to Twitch Affiliates and Partners Only

If you wish to join the Twitch Affiliate Program, you need to meet the following criteria:

- Stream for at least eight hours in the last 30 days
- Steam on at least seven days in the last 30 days
- Receive an average of three viewers per stream
- Grow your audience to 50 followers

If you meet these criteria, Twitch automatically invites you to become an Affiliate.

Twitch offers you a few additional earning opportunities as an affiliate. These are still available should you manage to make the jump from Affiliate to Partner.

## Twitch Bits

Twitch Bits are effectively mini-donations from viewers. They pay for them using either Amazon Payments or PayPal. Bits are a type of virtual currency that gamers can "spend" on their favourite gamers' sites. Twitch pays their Affiliates and Partners one cent for every Bit fans use on their channels.

A viewer can Cheer with his Bits. When a viewer Cheers, he uses his Bits to pay for the right to participate in a chat on a particular gamer's chat channel. He can also use Bits to buy emotes he can use in the chat – with the bigger, more animated emotes costing more Bits. A viewer earns a Cheer Chat Badge in any gamer's chat channel in which he participates. The more a viewer chats in a channel, the more Bits he spends, and over time he can earn a better Cheer Chat Badge.

You can set the minimum number of Bits needed to send a Cheer message in your channel, so people don't spam your chat with multiple uses of single Bits. Likewise, you can set the smallest emote somebody can use in your channel.

You can also add a StreamLabs Tip Jar widget to your stream. This shows an image of an empty glass filling up as people use Bits on your channel. This helps encourage your followers to use more Bits to "fill up" your glass.

## Twitch Subscriptions

Twitch Subscriptions provide a recurring income to streamers. You can encourage your followers to subscribe to your channel for either $US4.99, $9.99 or $24.99 per month. The money collected is split 50/50 between Twitch and the streamer (although a few top streamers have been able to negotiate a higher percentage).

As soon as you sign up as an Affiliate or Partner, a Subscribe button will automatically appear on your page. Streamers can set up alerts to encourage gamers to subscribe. These are signs that pop up on the screens saying that somebody has bought (or renewed their subscription) to your channel. These are particularly popular with Twitch users who love to see their name on their favourite gamer's page.

# Income Sources Available to Twitch Partners Only

Twitch targets its Partner program at the platform's best streamers. Unlike the Affiliate program, the Twitch Partnership program is exclusive - invitation only. You can start the process by requesting they consider you, however.

There is no published criteria on how Twitch selects partners. They do admit, however, that the following factors affect their evaluation:

Content – Twitch expects their partners to produce the best possible content for their audience.

Average concurrent viewership – channels with high viewing levels are more likely to be offered an opportunity as a Twitch Partner. However, Twitch takes notice of your behavior and interaction with your community, both on Twitch, and other social platforms.

Stream frequency and schedule – Twitch expects their partners to broadcast at least three times per week at scheduled times.

There are a few additional ways that Partners can make money on Twitch on top of all of the other sources.

## Selling Games, In-Game Items, and T-Shirts

Twitch Partners can sell games and in-game items from their page. They can receive a 5% share of the revenue.

If a Partner plays a game which Twitch either sells or has in-game items to sell, a sales box automatically appears on their page below the video screen. If one of your viewers clicks on the box and makes a purchase, you will receive 5% of the revenue. This is automatic and requires no input from the Partner.

Although the sales box appears on the pages of all streamers who play relevant games, only Partners receive a portion of the proceeds. Partners can also sell t-shirts in the official Twitch t-shirt store.

## Video Ads

Twitch Partners can opt to run ads on their steam. They can select how often they want ads to run, as long as they leave at least eight minutes between commercials, as well as ad length, (from 30 seconds to 3 minutes). Partners share advertising revenue with Twitch. The more money Twitch receives from advertisers, the more they pay you.

Twitch pays you a flat-rate CPM (cost per 1000 views). The CPM changes depending on the time of year. Gaming companies happily pay more for ads at certain times, for instance during holiday seasons or when a product launch. A typical payment is $1 to $2 per thousand views.

You can choose from pre-roll, mid-roll, or post-roll ads. You should probably experiment to see which types of ads resound best with your audience.

Many Twitch broadcasters prefer to bypass using video ads. They realize how much their fans dislike ads, and they can make sufficient money from the other less intrusive income sources on Twitch.

# **CHAPTER EIGHT**

## **How to Earn Money from YouTube Channel**

Now you can utilize YouTube for both following your passion and feeding your wallet. In this section, we are going to discuss how to make money from YouTube. Stay with us!

## **Who Can Upload Videos on YouTube?**

You can watch innumerable videos on YouTube without doing registration. However, if you want to upload any video on YouTube you have to register through your Gmail account, which will take less than a minute. As a registered user, you can upload as many video contents as you want. You can also communicate with our subscribers through comments.

Now what kind of contents can you upload to YouTube? This American video sharing platform allows diverse contents including short original videos, TV show clips, audio recordings, video blogging, music videos, live streams, educational videos, documentary films, video clips, short films, movie trailers, etc. However, if any of your uploaded content is considered as potentially inappropriate, then it would be visible only to registered users aged 18 years or older.

## Set Up YouTube Channel

Opening a YouTube channel is like building a doorway to earn from YouTube. One YouTube channel is attached with every YouTube account. Like Google account, a YouTube account grants you access to the Google products, like Gmail, Google Drive, etc.

Now how to open an account on YouTube? If you have a Google account, then you can directly 'Sign In' on YouTube using your Gmail account. Otherwise, you need to open a Google account. Let's see the account opening process in different mediums.

## Add Valuable Content

Your earning mostly depends on the quality of your uploaded content on your YouTube channel. Try to focus on the quality of your content. The length of video may vary considering the type of content you want to upload. But it would be wise, not making the contents too lengthy.

Your content may not be perfect at first, try to upgrade the quality. However, practice can make your videos perfect. If you put effort to make each content better than the previous one, you will certainly learn and improve as you go.

To ameliorate the quality and resolution of your videos, use better tools and equipment like advanced camera, latest video editing software, etc. You can also learn smart filming techniques to upgrade the way you film. For instance, to employ more lights into your scenes, you can place the camera on a tripod. In simple words, your YouTube channel will thrive if you can produce high-end videos.

The frequency of Content Uploading is another important issue for gaining success in YouTube. Try to stay consistent in uploading contents on your YouTube channel; otherwise people will forget you. If you want more people to subscribe your YouTube channel, maintain a strict schedule for adding content and stick to it.

The audience will more likely to find your channel on YouTube, if you can follow some simple but effective Search Engine Optimization (SEO) techniques to draw people (web traffic) to your video directly from organic YouTube search results. First, add a proper description of your video that best describes your content. Second, tag your uploaded content with proper keywords.

## Grab Audience

Not to mention, connecting with a bigger audience is the key to monetize your YouTube channel. The open secret to get more subscribers is to upload top-quality content in your YouTube channel complying with YouTube rules. Quality contents will keep the audience returning to your YouTube channel. As we have mentioned before, uploading content regularly is quite effective to hold the audience on any YouTube channel.

To increase the popularity of your YouTube channel among the audience, try to keep interaction with the subscribers through replying to their remarks. Follow the comments (both positive and negative) and questions of the subscribers to know what they like/don't like. Making videos based on user interest is another great way to hook the audience on your YouTube channel.

To attract more audience, you can share/embed your video contents on popular social media networks like Twitter, Linked In, Facebook, etc. The more you share or embed the content links on the internet, the greater chance to get subscribers on your channel and earn money.

## Channel Monetization through YouTube Partner Program (YPP)

You can earn money from YouTube staying anywhere on earth. All you need is a stable internet connection and access to a valid Gmail account. In this section, we will discuss how to earn from YouTube. You can monetize your YouTube channel through several ways. Let's talk about the most popular way of channel monetization. It is termed as "YouTube Partner Program (YPP)".

## YPP Monetization Requirements

To avail the opportunity of YouTube Monetization through YouTube Partner Program (YPP), you need to fulfil some requirements. On 16th January 2018, YouTube declared the latest eligibility requirements for YPP from any YouTube channel.

**Your channel must have a minimum 1,000 subscribers.**

Your channel must have minimum 4,000 hours (2,40,000 minutes) of watch time within the past 12 months

Your channel must comply with YouTube Terms of Service, YouTube Partner Program policies, Community Guidelines, and YouTube spam policies.

## How to Check the Total Number of Subscribers

To start earning from your YouTube videos, you need to enable monetization in your YouTube channel. First go to youtube.com. Then, sign in to your YouTube account and click on your Profile icon on the top right corner. A drop-down list will appear where you will find a button called "Your Channel". Clicking on this button, you can see the total number of subscribers of your channel. If your channel has got at least 1000 subscribers, then you have passed the first requirement of YouTube monetization.

## How to Check the Total Watch Time

To check the total number of "watch hours" you need to navigate to the analytics section of your YouTube channel. Inside your channel page, you will find the button "Creator Studio". Now if you click on this button, the system will take you to the content list of your channel. On the left side bar, you will find "Analytics" button. Here you will find two options: "Stay on Classic Analytics" and "Go to New Analytics".

Clicking on the "Classic Analytics", you will enter a new page. Here you can see the lifetime analytics of your channel. Using the filter option, you can see the total "watch hour" of your channel in the last 12 months. To fulfil the second requirement of YouTube Monetization, your channel needs at least 240000 minutes (4000 hours) of watch time in the last 12 months.

## How to Check Channel Strike Status

According to YPP rules, your channel must not contain any video which has violated YouTube Terms of Service, YouTube Partner Program policies, Community Guidelines, and YouTube spam policies. Now how to check whether your channel is free from any policy violation strike?

In your YouTube Channel Page, you will find the "Channel" button on the left sidebar. Clicking on this button, you will reach a new page titled "Status and Features" showing overall status of your channel. Check the "Copyright Status" and "Community Guideline Status". If there is any strike, it would be visible on the respective status bar.

**Set up Google AdSense.**

Inside the "Status and Features" page you will find a section called "Monetization", below the Copyright and Community Guideline Status Bars. The "Monetization" section will show a button called "Enable". Now click on this button, which will take you to the "Monetization" page. Here you fill some terms and conditions. After reading those terms click on the "Start" button. Now the system will take you to a new page titles "Apply for Monetization". Reading the provided terms and conditions, click on the "I Accept" button.

Returning back to the "Monetization" page, you will find an option called "Sign Up for AdSense". Click on the "Start" button and after that click on the "Next" button. Now the system will take you to AdSense website. Opening an AdSense account is mandatory to earn from YPP; because the earning will be directly deposited into your AdSense account. Setting up an AdSense account is totally free. All you need is a Gmail account. For opening an AdSense account, you can either insert the same Gmail account used for opening your YouTube account or use a new Gmail account.

On the "Google AdSense | Sign Up" page, your channel's URL Link would be visible automatically. From the drop-down list, choose the country where you live. Then, read the AdSense terms and conditions. Reading those clauses, accept the agreement and click on the "Create Account" button at the end of this page. Now you have successfully created an AdSense account.

Note that you must be at least 18 years of old to create an AdSense account. However, if your age is below 18 years, you can take the help of an adult for AdSense account creation.

## Insert Your Payment Details

Now a window will appear showing "Get Started" button. Click on this button. At this step, the system will require you to fulfil the form titled "Payment Address Details". Input your Name, Address and Contact number.

Here you need to remember several things. First, use the same name you have used in your bank; otherwise you might face severe difficulty later. Second, insert the proper address of your home, as Google AdSense will send a letter with verification PIN at your address when your channel earns $10. Next, use a valid phone number.

When you click on the "Submit" button the system will show you a redirection window. Clicking on "Redirection" button the system will again take you to Your YouTube channel's "Monetization" Page.

## Set Monetization Preferences

On the "Monetization" Page, you will see four options. Here the 3rd option is "Set Monetization Preferences". Clicking on the "Start" button, you can see the available options for ads, including "Display Ads", "Overlay Ads", "Sponsored Ads", and "Skippable Video Ads". Choose the most suitable type of ads for your contents and click on the "Save" button. Now your channel is sent for review.

## Review Process

When you have submitted your YouTube channel for YPP monetization, it will go under review. A review team will visit your channel and analyse whether your channel fulfils the YPP Monetization Requirement. The YPP review team will also check whether your contents are unique and free from copyright issues. The YPP review process might take one week to six months. After reviewing, YouTube might approve or reject your Channel for YPP monetization. If your channel gets approved under YouTube Partner Program (YPP), you will get an email from YouTube.

YouTube is the most popular video sharing platform in today's world. Here people can share their own videos, create a fan base and earn money. So far, we have discussed the overall process of monetizing your YouTube channel through the YouTube Partnership Program. First, you need to create your YouTube account and set up your YouTube channel. Next, add valuable content to your channel to connect with the audience. Then, check out the Analytics, whether your channel has fulfilled the YPP monetization requirements. If your channel gets a minimum 1000 subscribers along with a minimum 4000 hours watch time (in last 12 months) and there is no strike for YouTube Policy violation, then you can enable the YPP monetization process. For that you need to apply to Google AdSense program, add payment details and select your preferred ad types to submit your channel for YPP Monetization review. If everything goes well, you will get an acceptance email from YouTube. On the whole, you need to upload quality products, to connect with more audiences and earn a handsome amount per month. Happy YouTubing!

# CHAPTER NINE

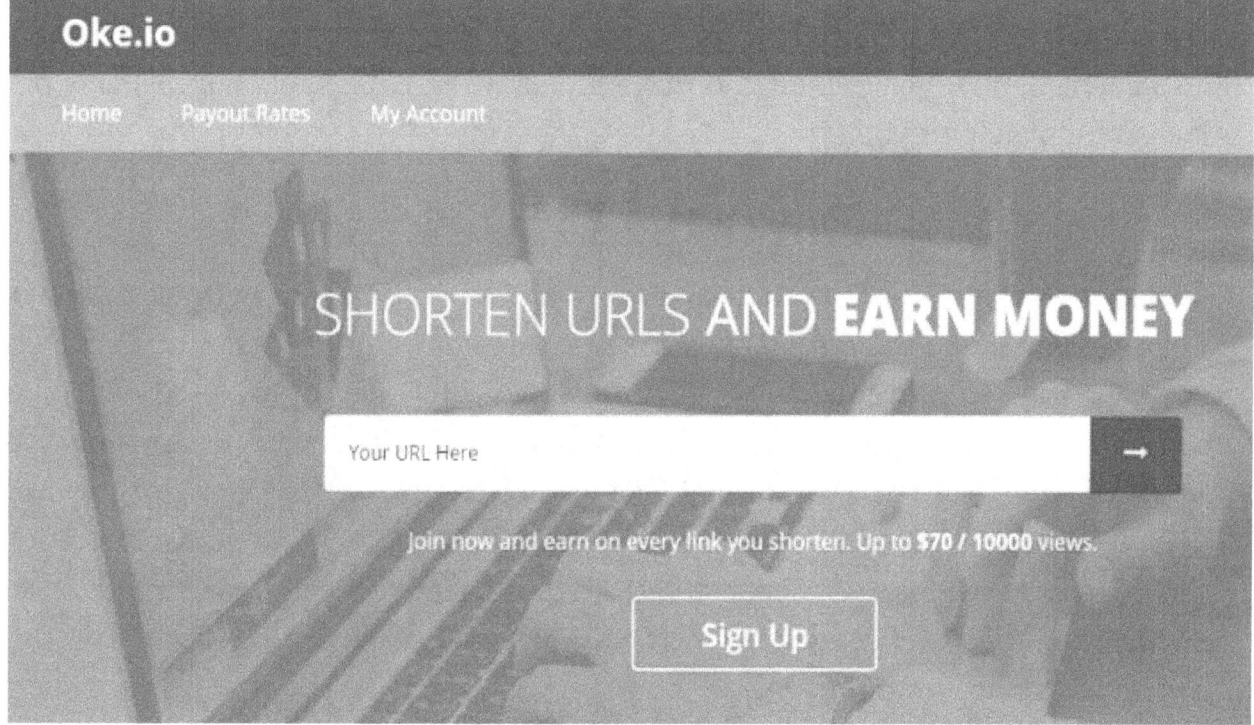

## How to monetize OKE.IO

Oke.io is one of the trusted link shortener service, here publishers can shorten their long URLs and they can earn money by using those shorten links. Okeio offers an opportunity to online users to earn money by sharing their shorten links. If you don't know anything about link shortener and earning methods from them, let me explain brief, If you short any long URL links to tiny URLs with Oke.io tools, then those shorten links contain some interstitial advertisement, if visitors clicks on that URL link then, he or she will see the advertisement for 5 seconds before redirecting to destination page. After 5 seconds of advertisement visitor will see the "Skip Ad" option, if he clicks on that, then visitor will be redirected destination page. Then publishers will be paid some amount for this process, payout rate is depending on visitor's nation.

Okeio is a new link shortener company. It has more than 18550 registered users all over the world. Oke.io offers some of the best features to its users to earn more, which are Low Minimum Payout, 24/7 Customer Support, Daily Payments, Counts Raw Traffic, Detailed Stats reporting system, Multiple Tools, High Payout Rates, Multiple Payment Options. This URL shortener service provides high payout rates to its users, while writing this post it was paying Up to $ 7.2 and its minimum payout rate is $ 2.4 for 1000 views. It counts up to 3x views from same person is also counted, so if you planning to make money from URL shortener this network is the best match for you.

## How Oke.io works?

Oke.io works same like shorte.st and adfly, now i will explain with an example. Let's say you like **abcdefghijkl#####url.com** and you want to share it with friends also you want to earn money by doing this. To earn money, you used Oke.io to shorten from **abcdefghijkl#####url.com/okeio- review-shortenurls-earn-html to http://Oke.io/###**. Then you placed Oke.io shorten link on facebook or twitter or your website. Then your friends and viewers click on your Oke.io shorten URL link, later he will see 5 seconds of advertisement. then it will redirect to **abcdefghijkl#####url.com/okeio- review-shortenurls-earn-html**. Then you will earn some money for doing this.

## How much does Oke.io pay you?

This URL shortener service provides high payout rates to its users, while writing this post it was paying Up to $ 7.2 and its minimum payout rate is $ 2.4 for 1000 views. It counts up to 3x views from same person is also counted, so if you planning to make money from URL shortener this network is best match for you. Its minimum cash out limit is only $ 5 and it uses 4 different payment methods to pay all its users on time, which are PayPal, Bitcoin, Skrill and Payza. Oke.io pays on daily basis to all its publishers on time. Okeio referral program is very attractive like shorte.st, adfly, short.pe etc. currently it offers 20% referral commission for life.

## Re□uirements and Restrictions:

- Don't advertise oke.io on PTC websites.

- Do not place Oke.io shortened URLs links on sites containing pornography or viruses etc.
- Don't offer an incentive to your visitor to click on your Oke.io tiny URL links to earn.
- Do not spam any forum with Oke.io URLs.
- Don 't use Oke.io service for any illegal purpose.
- Do not create multiple account with Oke.io.
- Don't click on your own oke.io shorten links.
- Don't send fake traffic to your oke.io links.
- Don't create redirect loop.
- Do not shorten any website if it is containing any illegal content

## Advertising Formats and Detailed Stats

Like other network Oke.io also provides banner based interstitial ads to its users. This link shortening site provides an advanced stat reporting system, here you can see, views, date, daily CPM, Announcements, earnings, total views, referral earnings, average CPM, total earnings, top 10 performing links, Link Earnings, referral earnings with graph.

## Payment Information

- Oke.io process payments on daily basis
- Publishers receives pay-outs on time from Oke.io
- Oke.io's minimum payment limit is only $ 5
- Oke.io uses PayPal, Skrill, Payza, Bitcoin as payment methods to pay.
- It provides Up to $ 7.2 as payout rate for 1000 views.
- Oke. io's minimum payout rate is $ 2.4 for 1000 visits.
- Publishers will get 20% referral commission.
- This URL shortener uses CPC and CPM as payment models.

# **CONCLUSION**

By far the biggest challenge of social media monetization is being heard through all the noise. You're also entirely at the mercy of the platform.

Having a private community can help you overcome the limitations and uncertainties of social media and the monetization opportunities that come with them. With a private and, preferably, mobile-centric online community, you have complete control over your own social space, and that means higher engagement too. There's no denying that private communities are the way of the future.

Disciple community management platform helps people build independent, valuable, and trusted communities in a safe space that they own and control. Choose from subscriptions, sponsorship, and in-app purchases to monetize your content and expertise. Create your own community space today.

www.ingramcontent.com/pod-product-compliance
Lightning Source LLC
Chambersburg PA
CBHW081459220526
45466CB00008B/2710